THE WHO TRIVIA BOOK

Uncover The History & Facts Every Fan Needs To Know!

By Dale Raynes

Bridge Press
support@bridgepress.org

Please consider writing a review!
Just visit: purplelink.org/review

Copyright 2021. Bridge Press. All Rights Reserved.

ISBN: 978-1-955149-23-5

TABLE OF CONTENTS

INTRODUCTION

Ever since they burst onto the rock scene in the mid-1960s, there has been something utterly unique about The Who. Others sang about rebellion, but this band *was* rebellion. Roger Daltrey yelled, "I hope I die before I get old." Pete Townshend bashed his guitar into the floor, and Keith Moon literally blew up his drums on more than one occasion. Meanwhile, John Entwistle was the real rocker in the band. Don't believe me? He died in Vegas at 57, with a groupie in his bed and cocaine on the bedstand.

Yet somehow, The Who was not a parody of rock chaos and debauchery. They grew into the most sophisticated and articulate band of their time. Pete wrote more than one award-winning rock opera and produced poignant and insightful songs on growing old and social issues. Through it all, The Who rocked. Only this remarkable band could invent the concept album, pioneer heavy metal, and still maintain the respect of punk rockers through their brute nihilism and dedication to aggressive music and self-destructive behavior.

Just listen to a masterwork like "Won't Get Fooled Again." No other band could combine a nuanced analysis of the political blowback that historically accompanies political revolutions with the hardest rocking riffage imaginable. Some died before they got old, and others didn't. There will never be another band like them.

The Who have a legacy worth exploring. Let's see how well you know these four lads from London who changed rock forever.

CHAPTER 1:

EARLY YEARS

1. Pete's father was an accomplished musician who played for the Royal Air Force Band. Which instrument did he play?
   a. Drums
   b. Saxophone
   c. Piano
   d. Trumpet

2. As a child, what was Pete's favorite escape from reality?
   a. Playing soccer
   b. Collecting stamps
   c. Going to the movies
   d. Reading adventure novels

3. Which '50s rocker got young Pete into rock 'n' roll?
   a. Little Richard
   b. Bill Hayley
   c. Jerry Lee Lewis
   d. Buddy Holly

4. Pete's brothers have an amusing combination of names. What is it?
    a. Paul and Simon
    b. George and Michael
    c. Ricky and Martin
    d. Bob and Dylan

5. Three of the four founding members of the band went to Acton County Grammar School together. Which member did not attend that school as a child?
    a. Keith Moon
    b. Roger Daltrey
    c. Pete Townshend
    d. John Entwistle

6. Keith came from another part of London. Which part of the city was it?
    a. Camden
    b. Greenwich
    c. Chelsea
    d. Wembley

7. True or False: Keith was a gifted artist as a child.

8. Roger was expelled from Acton County Grammar School. What did he do after he left?
    a. Formed his first band
    b. Joined a gang
    c. Started working construction
    d. Worked at a gas station

9. What was the name of the first band Pete and John ever formed together?
   a. The Dunces
   b. The Confederates
   c. The Rockefellers
   d. The Nantuckets

10. In 1959, Roger formed the band that would eventually become The Who. What were they called initially?
    a. The Detours
    b. The High Numbers
    c. The Rebel Rousers
    d. The Fentones

11. True or False: Pete was the leader of the band from the very beginning.

12. True or False: Pete came up with the name The Who after being inspired at art school.

13. As you would expect, Keith broke the drum set at his audition for the band. What did the band do in response?
    a. Billed him for the drums
    b. Hired him but warned him it must never happen again
    c. Hired him and commended him for his enthusiasm
    d. Hired someone else

14. The band changed their name to The High Numbers
and released a few singles to appeal to the mod
fashion craze in England at the time. Whose idea
was that?
    a. Pete's
    b. Roger's
    c. Keith's
    d. Their manager's

15. Pete admits to ripping off the windmill motion
from another guitarist. Who was it?
    a. Keith Richards
    b. Brian Jones
    c. Eric Clapton
    d. George Harrison

16. In June 1964, Pete first broke a guitar in concert.
Why did he do it?

    a. To attack an audience member trying to get on
        stage
    b. As a gimmick for a film
    c. The roof was too low
    d. He was playing it too hard

17. Pete wanted the band to sign with the manager of
The Kinks, Shel Talmy. Therefore, he wrote a song
that was intended to sound like The Kinks. What
was the song?
    a. "Anyway, Anyhow, Anywhere"
    b. "Can't Explain"

c. "My Generation"
d. "The Kids Are Alright"

18. True or False: "I Can't Explain" was about drugs.

19. After the band got signed, they switched to writing their own materials. However, one member was unhappy and wanted to continue to record and play R&B and Motown covers. Which member wanted The Who to be a cover band?
a. Roger Daltrey
b. John Entwistle
c. Keith Moon
d. Pete Townshend

20. True or False: The Who identified deeply with the mod fashion movement.

ANSWERS

1. B. Saxophone. Cliff Townshend was the alto saxophonist for the military Squadronaires band — not a bad job to have in World War II! Later on, he had a fairly big hit with an instrumental version of the Righteous Brothers song, "Unchained Melody." Meanwhile, Pete's mother was a singer with the Sydney Torch and Les Douglass Orchestras.

2. D. Reading adventure novels. His favorites were Gulliver's Travels and Treasure Island.

3. B. Bill Hayley. He saw *Rock Around the Clock*, the first rock 'n roll movie, which featured Bill Hayley and the Comets. Not long after that, Pete saw Hayley play in the first concert he ever attended.

4. A. Paul and Simon. Obviously, they were not aware of the American songwriter (who was already musically active, by the way) at the time.

5. A. Keith Moon. At the time, it was a school for children aged 11 to 18. But in 1967, it became a comprehensive school.

6. D. Wembley.

7. False. Art is subjective, but his teacher certainly didn't think so. His report card said that he was, "Retarded artistically. Idiotic in other respects."

8. C. Started working construction. If you said that he joined a gang, you are not wholly wrong. That was one of the reasons he was expelled. Roger called his autobiography *Thanks a Lot, Mr. Kibblewhite: My Story.* It is named after the teacher who expelled Roger. "It had probably been on the cards for a while," the singer remembers, "I'd been caught smoking. I'd been caught playing truant. I was disruptive in class because I just wanted to be left alone by these teachers."

9. B. The Confederates. Yes, it was an unfortunate name. The band was a trad-jazz group, but Pete began to lose interest as he got more into rock 'n roll. Pete left the band after getting into a fight withits drummer.

10. A. The Detours. The High Numbers was a later name. The other two are acts The Detours opened for and by whom they were influenced.

11. False. There is general agreement that Roger was the leader at first. According to Pete, Daltrey "ran things the way he wanted them." Pete also claimed in his autobiography that Roger was the "undisputed leader of the band." However, that latter statement seems vastly exaggerated and modest on the part of Townshend.

12. False. Or, not exactly. Pete and his roommate, Richard Barnes, spent the night brainstorming

ideas. Pete's favorite was The Hair. Barnes preferred The Who. Daltrey selected The Who out of the candidates. We are left to imagine Tommy as performed by The Hair.

13. C. Hired him and commended him for his enthusiasm.

14. D. The idea was put forward by their manager, Peter Meaden. However, the singles they released in a naked attempt to appeal to the mod crowd did not chart. The single "Zoot Suit/I'm the Face" does make for amusing listening nowadays.

15. A. Keith Richards. Pete saw Keith do it in one of the early Rolling Stones shows and loved it. When he saw that Richards did not repeat it later, Pete adopted it as his own. Tupported the stones the Stones for two shows. As Pete later recalled, "they were young, they were brand new, and they had one hit, with a Chuck Berry song called, 'Come On.' I met them backstage, and they were all very charming. As the curtain opened, Keith Richards is doing this [the guitarist relates, standing up and demonstrating the wind-mill motion]." However, when Pete asked the young Keith about it, he denied having ever done that. So, Townshend figured he could freely adopt the motion.

16. C. The roof was too low. Then the audience started laughing, immensely annoying Pete. Therefore, he

smashed the guitar into smithereens and just picked up a new one. A legend was born. *Rolling Stone* called the moment, which occurred at the Railway Hotel in Harrow, one of "50 Moments that Changed the History of Rock and Roll." While most people thought of the smashing as a visual element, Roger believes it was a sonic one. "They didn't get it. It was not about the visual of it. It was about the sound it made. When Pete used to break a guitar, it sometimes used to take him ten minutes. It would be like a sacrificial lamb. This thing would scream. It was an incredible sonic experience. The volume would leave us with our ears bleeding. Sometimes we used to come off stage, and the ringing in our ears didn't go away for two days."

17. B. "I Can't Explain." It certainly worked. Talmy came to rehearsals and was impressed, signing the band and taking them under his wing. As Roger explained, "We already knew Pete could write songs, but it never seemed a necessity in those days to have your own stuff because there was this wealth of untapped music that we could get hold of from America. But then bands like The Kinks started to make it, and they were probably the biggest influence on us — they were certainly a huge influence on Pete, and he wrote 'I Can't Explain,' not as a direct copy, but certainly it's very derivative of Kinks music."

18. True. While a love song on the surface, it alludes to drugs in more than one way. Pete says it was about a guy who "can't tell his girlfriend he loves her because he's taken too many Dexedrine tablets." Indeed, the song describes some of the symptoms of using amphetamines, which is why he was "dizzy in the head" and "hot and cold."

19. Roger Daltrey. Luckily, he was outvoted by the other band members. He had the band record another session of R&B covers which remained unreleased.

20. False. Pete says that to a certain extent, the band was using the mod aesthetic to sell records and gain recognition. "I think people tended to see us in those days through the lens of the documentaries and the way the history was documented, but The Who were not really part of the mod movement, the mod movement was our support system," adds Townshend. "We were able to observe it and use it and ride on it, and we were supported, as long as we stuck to a fairly straightened set of rules. One was that it was mainly a male audience, so we had to be pretty brutal, and then, there was the fact that we also had to have our hair short and not look scruffy like the Rolling Stones, and not care whether girls screamed at us like they did at The Beatles. And so, for a while, we tried to look like our audience. But then after a while, we realized that it was colorless."

DID YOU KNOW?

- Pete Townshend wrote about sexual abuse in songs like "Cousin Kevin" and "Fiddling About" because he had experienced it as a child. In 2017, Pete stopped playing those songs after almost having a nervous breakdown when playing them. His parents were an unstable couple, and he lived with his grandmother. He wrote that she "took in men from the bus garage and the railway station opposite her flat all the time." She seems to have allowed at least one of these men to abuse him. Pete later said that the time at his grandmother's house "is the only bit of my life that I haven't beenable to make any sense of. If I was able to go into regressive hypnosis and either find some terrible trauma or nothing at all, it would be equally damaging to me as an artist."

- He also perfected his famous guitar smashing technique in response to his abusive grandmother. Pete and John Entwistle were practicing in his room when, as Pete describes it, she came in screaming, "Turn that f***ing row down!" Then, "I did a Keith Moon — long before I'd ever met Keith Moon. 'You think that's a f***ing row? Listen to this!' And I got my guitar and smashed it over the amplifier." Luckily, he only lived with her for two years.

- Roger can't remember as much as he would like about his childhood because he has experienced four concussions. Roger says he realized how bad it had gotten when he was writing his autobiography. "The scariest thing about the memoir is that I have had four serious concussions in my life. There are huge gaps, and I wonder why. But there is no wonder why."

- Daltrey was a very violent kid from a working-class neighborhood. His violent streak got him fired from the band very early on. In one show, Moon played poorly. Roger blamed the drummer's methamphetamine habit and threw out Keith's stash. When Moon confronted the singer, holding a tambourine, he got punched in the face. Roger recalled, "It took about five people to hold me off him. It wasn't just because I hated him, it was just because I loved the band so much and thought it was being destroyed by those pills." John and Pete knew Roger for longer, but they took Keith's side and fired Roger from the band. It was managers Kit Lambert and Chris Stamp who convinced the band to reconcile with Roger.

- The Who's sound was different from the other British invasion bands. It was more chaotic and violent. Pete credits that with the atmosphere he grew up in. The trauma of World War II, a war that ended around when the guitarist was born, was very significant in his life. "When I was four I lived in a house where 12 people had died. We played in bomb sites, we'd find bits of bodies, skeletons, and watches every day." Pete believes this darkness and violence is what made the music of The Who so unique. "Trauma is passed from generation to generation. I've unwittingly inherited what my father experienced."

CHAPTER 2:

EARLY SUCCESS AND UNFORGETTABLE SINGLES

1. The Who was not played on BBC in their early years. However, they were a smash hit on pirate radio. Which station was mainly instrumental in their breaking out?
   a. Radio Caroline
   b. Radio London
   c. Radio Luxembourg
   d. Radio Jackie

2. True or False: The song, "Anyway, Anyhow, Anywhere," was rejected by the record company because it included feedback noises.

3. Which label released early The Who singles in the United Kingdom?
   a. Decca
   b. EMI

    c. Brunswick
    d. Capitol

4. The album *My Generation* includes two cover versions of songs from which soul giant?
    a. Ray Charles
    b. James Brown
    c. Sam Cooke
    d. Jackie Wilson

5. When Roger sings the song, "My Generation," he famously stutters during the verse. Why did the band include that in the song?
    a. It was a mistake but it sounded cool
    b. They imitated another hit song
    c. It was supposed to express the inarticulation of a generation
    d. It was a tribute to how people sounded on amphetamines

6. Which song, appearing on the UK version of the *My Generation* album, was cut from the American release for its sexual content?
    a. "The Ox"
    b. "I'm a Man"
    c. "Please, Please, Please"
    d. "I Don't Mind"

7. What song recorded during the *My Generation* sessions featured rhythm guitar from Jimmy Page, the future guitarist of Led Zeppelin?

a. "Bald Headed Woman"
b. "A Legal Matter"
c. "Circles"
d. "Anytime You Want Me"

8. True or False: When Jeff Beck got Keith to play on his classic song, "Beck's Bolero," he was trying to convince him to leave The Who.

9. "A Quick One, While He's Away," is one of the most important rock songs of the '60s. It essentially invented the rock-opera genre. Why was it written?
   a. It was Pete's art school pet project
   b. The band was trying to keep up with The Beatles
   c. To prove to the BBC that the band was serious artists
   d. They had a lot of time to fill on their album

10. In 1967, The Who had a hit single with the song, "Pictures of Lily." Who was that song written about?
    a. A fictional character
    b. Lili Damita
    c. Lilly Langtry
    d. Lillian Baylis

11. What was The Who's first No. 1 single in the United Kingdom?
    a. "I Can't Explain"
    b. "My Generation"

c. "Substitute"
    d. "I'm a Boy"

12. What was the only top 10 single the band had in the United States?
    a. "My Generation"
    b. "I Can See For Miles"
    c. "Happy Jack"
    d. "Pinball Wizard"

13. A Motown classic inspired the single, "Substitute." Which song got Pete's creative juices going?
    a. "Not Too Proud to Beg"
    b. "Stop! In the Name of Love"
    c. "Ain't No Mountain High Enough"
    d. "The Tracks of My Tears"

14. On the hit single, "Happy Jack," three band members share the vocal duties. Which member *doesn't* sing on the track?
    a. Pete
    b. Roger
    c. John
    d. Keith

15. True or False" On the mini-opera, "A Quick One, While He's Away," the band featured a cello part for the first and last time.

16. Which of The Who's early album releases featured a picture of the band standing with Big Ben in the background?
    a. *My Generation* (UK version)
    b. *The Who Sings My Generation* (US version)
    c. *Ready Steady Who*
    d. *Happy Jack*

17. The Who had more than one residency at the legendary Marquee Club in London. In what year did they perform their last residence there?
    a. 1964
    b. 1965
    c. 1966
    d. 1967

18. True or False: John Entwistle played the solo on the song, "Substitute."

19. Why did the band record the two Rolling Stones singles, "The Last Time" and "Under My Thumb," and release them as a single?
    a. Pete loved the songs
    b. The band believed they could record them better
    c. The band was low on material
    d. They wanted to support the release of Jagger and Richards from jail

20. John Entwistle's first song for the band was "Boris the Spider," the tragic story of a dead spider sung in a gruff bass voice. He came up with the idea during a drinking spree with which member of the Rolling Stones?
   a. Mick Jagger
   b. Keith Richards
   c. Bill Wyman
   d. Brian Jones

ANSWERS

1. A. Radio Caroline. The main avenue for broadcasting in the UK, the BBC, was known as "auntie" at the time. This was a poke at its tedious institutional nature.

2. True. It is hard to emphasize just how revolutionary the noisy and energetic material The Who was producing at the time was.

3. B. James Brown. The two songs were "I Don't Mind" and "Please, Please, Please." The latter song was a legendary one, which Roger did admirably. When Brown would perform that song, he went all out with theatrics, pretending to sing it until he collapsed from exhaustion, then being escorted off stage before bursting back to finish it.

4. C. Brunswick. They were a subsidiary of Decca that mostly sold American artists in the United Kingdom. They mainly specialized in R&B and soul artists. However, they were signed through Shel Talmy. Therefore, when the band fell out with him, they moved labels.

5. D. It was a tribute to how people sounded on amphetamines. Amphetamines were very popular with mods at that time, and that was their target

audience. In addition, some members took them quite often, most notably, Keith.

6. B. "I'm a Man," a strange choice since the Bo Diddley song was released in the United States previously, in the original version and as a Yardbirds cover version.

7. A. "Bald Headed Woman." Manager Shel Talmy wrote the song. Entwistle remembered, "The fuzz guitar droning throughout is played by Jimmy Page." "The reason being, he owned the only fuzz box in the country at that time."

8. True. Keith had just had one of his period bust-ups with Pete and had left the band in a huff. Jeff hoped to take advantage of that to get Keith to join his group. The song gives us an idea of how amazing that band would have sounded. Jimmy Page and John Paul Jones also took part in that session, with significant results for rock history. Keith said a band they started together would go down like a lead balloon, inspiring the legendary hard rock band Led Zeppelin.

9. D. They had a lot of time to fill on their album. Manager Kit Lambert encouraged Pete to fill the ten-minute gap with one long song rather than make three or four short pop songs. The end result was both glorious and ridiculous.

10. C. Lilly Langtry. Initially, Pete had said that the song was about a picture he had seen on his

girlfriend's wall. However, he later revealed it referenced a well-known actress and socialite who was also rumored to have been Edward VII's mistress. The story makes sense because Langtry died in 1929, like the Lily in the song.

11. Trick question. Amazingly, The Who has never had a No. 1 single in the UK, a fact Pete laughs about memorably on the *Live At Leeds* album. "I'm a Boy" and "My Generation" reached No. 2.

12. B. "I Can See for Miles."

13. D. "The Tracks of My Tears." The Smokey Robinson and the Miracles classic included the lines "Although she may be cute/She's just a substitute." The cutting phrase stuck in Pete's mind and inspired his memorable lyrics. The song came out during a very tense time in racial relations in the United States. Therefore, the line, "I look all white, but my dad was black" was altered, and Roger sings, "I try walking forward, but my feet walk back."

14. D. Keith. However, that did not stop him from trying to join in. If you listen to the song, you can hear Pete say, "I saw you!" when he caught Keith trying to join in against the band's orders.

15. False. Pete wrote a part for a cello, but their management could not afford it. Therefore, the band sensibly decided just to say "cello, cello, cello"

in the relevant part at the end of the "You Are Forgiven" mini-movement.

16. B. *The Who Sings My Generation* (US version). It was probably to make it clear to the American crowd that they were a British band and to capitalize on the success of the Stones and Beatles.

17. B. 1965. They grew a bit too big for the club after that. However, for nostalgic reasons, they played there again in 1967 and 1968. The Who was just one of the great bands to make their mark there, including the Rolling Stones, Fleetwood Mac, and the Yardbirds.

18. True. As John explained, "I played a Gibson SG medium scale bass with wire-wound strings. When it got to the solo, because we were recording and mixing it virtually live, I thought, yeah, this should be a bass solo, so I turned my volume up, and they couldn't mix me out, so it ended up as a bass solo."

19. D. They wanted to support the release of Jagger and Richards from jail. However, by the time the single was released, the duo had been released. The single was rushed out and did not even include Entwistle on bass.

20. C. Bill Wyman.

DID YOU KNOW?

- The band's best-known onstage behavior quirks, or gimmicks, as they were seen at the time, were developed in their earliest shows and are therefore an integral part of their identity. Roger would swing his microphone menacingly. Keith threw his drums in the air mid-beat and broke drum sets. At the same time, Pete made the famous wind-milling motion and used an immense amount of feedback. To Pete, some of these so-called gimmicks were as important as the music. He says, "I haven't smashed it, I've sculpted it for them ... I stumbled upon something more powerful than words, far more emotive than my white boy attempts to play the blues."

- Pete eventually resented being expected to smash his guitar all the time. He said about it, "It's also embarrassing, is what it is. It's like comedians being forced to use their catchphrase after they've become serious actors." However, the guitarist later made peace with the expectations. "Well, you have to remember I'm not angry all the time. Even now, I occasionally get frustrated on the stage with guitars and want to smash them. I tend not to do it, but the opportunity's always there. I smashed a guitar on the Psycho Derelict tour, and it was great fun."

- When Pete was fresh out of art school, he drove a Packard hearse around. For some reason, he loved the morbid car. However, when he moved to an apartment in Belgravia at 8 Chesham Place, Buckingham Palace became Pete's next-door neighbor. The Queen Mother (that is, Queen Elizabeth's mom) was unhappy about seeing Pete's strange car choice. "One day I came back and it was gone," he explained. "Apparently, her husband had been buried in a similar vehicle and it reminded her of him. But when I went to collect it, they wanted £250. And I'd only paid £30 for it in the first place." It had long been said that this experience inspired Pete to write the classic song "My Generation." However, this is not the case.

- Instead, the song was an expression of the frustration of an entire generation in the United Kingdom. The older British generation had experienced the war and felt they had sacrificed a lot for the younger generation. However, they were emotionally stunted and expected the youth of Britain to conform. This tension led to the explosion of counter-culture in England in the 1960s. As Pete explains, "Those people had sacrificed so much for us, but they weren't able to give us anything, no guidance, no inspiration, nothing really … We were expected to shut up and enjoy the peace. And we decided not to do that."

CHAPTER 3:

THE WHO SELLS OUT
AND *TOMMY*

1. True or False: The Who connected the songs with adverts and jingles because they did not have enough material for "The Who Sells Out" album.

2. True or False: "The Who Sells Out" came out when bands were releasing classic albums such as "Pet Sounds" and "Sgt. Peppers Lonely Hearts Club Band." However, Pete was determined to write a better album than the competition.

3. As The Who outgrew the mod scene, they became closely affiliated with the art pop movement, which exploded in London in the mid-60s. What was their relationship with the designers and artists on that scene?
   a. The Who were inspired by their designs
   b. The artists were inspired by The Who

    c. They worked closely together with the artists

    d. They grew separately around the same time

4. True or False: Pete believed that "I Can See for Miles" was his best song and was overjoyed when it became the band's most successful single up to that point.

5. In 1967, both the Jimi Hendrix Experience and The Who played the Monterey Pop Festival. Both were worried about following the other legendary act. How did they settle who would go first?

    a. Jimi graciously let The Who go first

    b. The Who graciously let Jimi go first

    c. It was settled in a physical fight

    d. They had a coin toss

6. After Jimi lost, he was concerned that he would be unable to top The Who's mayhem and destruction act. What did he do to top them?

    a. He focused on playing better

    b. He burned his guitar

    c. He also smashed his guitar

    d. He played with his guitar behind his back and with his teeth

7. Monterey launched The Who's bid to win over the United States. Which band did they tour with after that?

    a. The Beach Boys

    b. Herman's Hermits

c. The Monkees
d. The Archies

8. Moon celebrated his 21st birthday by reportedly driving a car into the pool of the band's hotel.Which hotel chain banned him for life as a result?
   a. The Hilton
   b. The Sheraton
   c. The Marriott
   d. The Holiday Inn

9. In 1968, the band had trouble with the authorities and press in a country they visited. Which country was it?
   a. Canada
   b. Australia
   c. New Zealand
   d. South Africa

10. The whimsical song, "Magic Bus," was a surprisingly big hit for the bad. Released as a single, Pete wrote it during the recording of which album?
    a. *My Generation*
    b. *A Quick One*
    c. *The Who Sells Out*
    d. *Tommy*

11. In the 1960s, it was very fashionable for rock stars to adopt an Indian guru as their spiritual guide. Who performed that role for Pete?

a. Maharishi Mahesh Yogi
b. Swami A.C. Bhaktivedanta Prabhupada
c. Merwan Sheriar Irani
d. Bhagwan Shree Rajneesh

12. The rock opera, *Tommy*, had several working names before they settled on the final one. Which of these was NOT one of those names?
    a. *Amazing Journey*
    b. *True Blindness*
    c. *The Brain Opera*
    d. *Omnibus*

13. *Tommy* is known as Pete's brainchild. However, John wrote a couple of the songs as well. Which of these songs was written by the bassist?
    a. "The Hawker"
    b. "Go to the Mirror!"
    c. "Smash the Mirror"
    d. "Fiddle About"

14. The song Sally Simpson is about a girl who is disfigured while trying to touch Tommy. It was based on violence Pete witnessed in a show by which band?
    a. The Rolling Stones
    b. The Doors
    c. Cream
    d. The Jimi Hendrix Experience

15. True or False: Despite the complexity of the material, the band finished recording in just ten days and was under budget.

16. The Who premiered *Tommy* live at a famous opera house and subsequently played it at several major ones in Europe. Where did they first play the rock opera?
    a. The Royal Concertgebouw, Amsterdam
    b. The Théâtre des Champs-Élysées, Paris
    c. The Royal Danish Theatre, Copenhagen
    d. Bayerisches Staatsoper, Munich

17. At Woodstock, Pete Townshend punched which iconic counter-culture figure for daring to come on stage while the band was performing?
    a. Allen Ginsberg
    b. Timothy Leary
    c. Abbie Hoffman
    d. Ken Kesey

18. True or False: Aside from the confrontation of the previous question, Pete also engaged in physical violence with other well-known people at Woodstock.

19. True or False: Everyone in the band, aside from Pete, tripped on acid at Woodstock.

20. During the band's performance at Woodstock, the sun famously rose right in the middle of what song?

a. "Pinball Wizard"
b. "My Generation"
c. "Heaven and Hell"
d. "See Me, Feel Me"

ANSWERS

1. False. Or, sort of false. Despite constantly playing live, Pete was on a writing spree. "I think I was just writing for myself and hoped that if I wrote maybe 20 or 30 or, on a good run, 40 pieces of music, at least 20 would get recorded, and then we could handpick maybe 10 to 12. For an album," he says. However, he was not very happy with the material he had. Townshend recalls, "It was like throwing shit at the wall."

2. False. Pete did not believe the band was able to produce anything in that league. Pete's friend and former roommate, Richard Barnes, recalls that the band's managers wanted him to write something more ambitious than he intended to. "The Beatles were in a class to themselves, and the Stones had their blues thing down, so first The Who went the Tamla-Motown route, but they needed to move on and develop," Barnes recalls. "Kit encouraged Pete to think in new and incredibly creative ways. His father was Constance Lambert [the British composer], and it was Kit's idea for Pete to try to write in an operatic way or to tackle concepts bigger than the three-minute pop song, which opened doors none of us even knew existed."

3. B. The artists were inspired by The Who. At least, that is how Pete remembers it. He says that "when we started our residency at the Marquee, we appeared with target t-shirts, Union Jack jackets, Chevrons. This was early, but not so early. We'd already had our incarnation as faux-Mods with [previous manager] Peter Meaden, as the High Numbers. This was when we became leaders of the field, in a fashion sense, because immediately, the people around us on Carnaby Street, who were observing us very closely, like Trisha Locke, who had been working for Mary Quant. She brought Mary and her husband to come and see us, and immediately, they started to cop some of our designs into their designs."

4. False. Pete did think it was his best song, and it did better than the other singles. But he still wasn't happy with its performance. "To me, it was the ultimate Who record, yet it didn't sell. I spat on the British record buyer." However, the song is an undisputed classic and inspired the Beatles' song, "Helter Skelter," among countless others.

5. D. They had a coin toss. Both acts saw it as a crucial element in breaking into the American market. Therefore, they weren't willing to back down. Roger said there was a jam session to decide who would go first, but Pete says that is wrong. "I've heard Roger talk about it as a jam session, but it

wasn't a jam session. It was just Jimi on a chair playing at me. Playing at me like 'Don't fuck with me, you little shit.'"

6. B. He burned his guitar. It's true that he also played with the guitar behind his back and with his teeth, but that was part of his regular act. The Who had to admit that Jimi got the best of them, and he received the headlines and momentum from the Monterey Festival. In 2008, that charred 1965 Fender Stratocaster sold for over $450,000.

7. B. Herman's Hermits. We are not sure who had that bright idea, but it made for some bizarre shows. However, Keith found kindred spirits in the funloving Hermans Hermits members and developed his practical joking to an art form at the time.

8. D. The Holiday Inn. Several people have claimed that Keith drove a Lincoln Continental into a Flint Township Holiday Inn pool, part of a drunken birthday celebration on August 23, 1967. Moon said, "I ran out, jumped into the first car I came to, which was a brand-new Lincoln Continental. It was parked on a slight hill, and when I took the handbrake off, it started to roll, and it smashed straight through this pool surround (fence), and the whole Lincoln Continental went into the (Holiday) Inn swimming pool, with me in it." While some have debunked the story, some witnesses insist the story is true to this day.

9. B and C. Australia and New Zealand. The biggest paper in Nez Zealand referred to the band as "unwashed, foul-smelling, booze-swilling no-hopers." Meanwhile, they were arrested in Melbourne and told never to return to Australia.

10. A. "My Generation." However, the band was not enthusiastic and did not record it until 1968, when they were low on material. It became a staple of their live show. However, the members had very different opinions about it. John said it was his least favorite song to play because the bass line was one note. Meanwhile, Pete says he loves the rhythm so much that it was his favorite song to perform.

11. C. Merwan Sheriar Irani, also known as the Meher Baba. It is hard to stress the importance of his teachings to Pete's spiritual development and the content of his work in those years. He says that when he wrote the song "See Me, Feel Me," Pete felt he was writing it directly to his spiritual guide.He even wrote an article for *Rolling Stone* called "In Love with Meher Baba." He said that he followed his teachings that, "drugs are harmful mentally, spiritually and physically." Indeed, this guru was one of the few who did not mince words and attacked the drug culture of the hippie and counter-culture movement.

12. B. *True Blindness.* Pete also called it *Deaf, Dumb, And Blind Boy*. Pete told a journalist at the time, "The

package I hope is going to be called "*Deaf, Dumb and Blind Boy.*" It's a story about a kid that's born deaf, dumb, and blind and what happens to him throughout his life ... But what it's really all about is the fact that ... he's seeing things basically as vibrations which we translate as music. That's really what we want to do, create this feeling that when you listen to the music you can actually become aware of the boy, and aware of what he is all about because we are creating him as we play." Indeed, he gave the entire plot away in that interview.

13. D. "Fiddle About." Of the songs mentioned, only "Go to the Mirror" and "Smash the Mirror!" were written by Pete. "The Hawker" was written by blues legend Sonny Boy Williamson II. Pete gave the two songs about child abuse to John, and he wrote "Fiddle About" and "Cousin Kevin." Pete later revealed that he did not want to deal with his own episodes of abuse.

14. B. The Doors. Pete saw a female fan get attacked by a security guard when she tried to touch Jim Morrison.

15. False. The process of recording the album was an absolute mess. The band took far longer than expected and had to go on tour in the middle so that they wouldn't go broke. Decca ran out of

patience as it had been an entire year since *The Who Sells Out* was released. Therefore, a rushed compilation called *Magic Bus: The Who on Tour* was released, which the band intensely disliked. The other guys in the band started to get impatient with Pete's perfectionism. John said, "we had to keep going back and rejuvenating the numbers ... it just started to drive us mad."

16. A. The Royal Concertgebouw, Amsterdam. However, not every opera house wanted to host the band. Tour manager Peter Rudge said at the time, "The European tour is very political. We were turned down in Austria, Italy, Switzerland and got the cold shoulder in Spain. We've been working on the tour for four or five months, and the Germans were very groovy, so were the Dutch. But for some of the others, it was a bit too much for them to contemplate The Who in their sacred opera houses. 'How can you suggest ... a long-haired pop group!'"

17. C. Abbie Hoffman. Abbie came on to the stage to protest that the festival was going on, although activist John Sinclair had been arrested. Abbie grabbed a microphone and yelled, "I think this is a pile of shit while John Sinclair rots in prison ..." Pete turned to look at Hoffman and shouted, "Fuck off! Fuck off my stage!" and according to witnesses, ran at Hoffman and hit him with his guitar on the back. Townshend said he did not do so because he

disagreed with Hoffman. Pete agreed that Sinclair should be released. However, he says that he would have knocked anyone off the stage due to the "sanctity of the stage." However, later both Hoffman and Townshend denied that the confrontation turned violent.

18. True. Before the show, Pete kicked Michael Wadleigh, the renowned Oscar-winning director and cinematographer of the Woodstock biopic. He did so to warn him to stay out of his way while shooting the band. The guitarist also finished the evening bashing his Gibson SG into the stage and tossing it into the crowd. It looks like Pete did not get in the spirit of peace and love that day.

19. False. Everyone in the band was tripping on acid, including the anti-drug Pete. The water supply had been filled with acid. Therefore, The Who were amongst many people who found themselves high on acid against their will. This unpleasantness contributed a great deal to the violent mood the band was in as they performed.

20. D. "See Me, Feel Me." The show was scheduled for a strange time slot, Sunday morning, August 17, 5:30–6:35 a.m. The band also had the misfortune of following Sly and the Family Stone and their legendary set. However, The Who held their own and put on a solid show. As the sun rose in the

dramatic climax of the song "See Me, Feel Me," a truly magical moment in music history unfolded. Entwistle said, "God was our lighting man."

41

DID YOU KNOW

- As a thank you to the pirate radio stations that had given the band the exposure it needed to make it, *The Who Sells Out* was a salute. The songs were held together by ads and spots mentioning pirate radio stations. Thus, the album sounded like one of the shows on a pirate radio station. "The BBC wasn't playing any tunes," Townshend says flatly at the memory. "Pirate radio was everything. It put us on the map in a big, big way. It helped everybody."

- *The Who Sells Out* is generally acknowledged as one of the great masterpieces of '60s rock. The band was mostly known for their live shows, and they toured relentlessly. However, Pete was dissatisfied with it. "The songs we recorded in the six months after the album came out were better," Townshend says. "If our label — who was also our managers, by the way — had just waited, maybe it could have been our greatest album. It's an interesting thought, isn't tit?"

- The Who were not a particularly tight-knit band. The personalities were just far too different, and they did not jell. Pete was the aloof and tortured intellectual. Roger was the pragmatic working-class kid with a temper. Keith was a self-destructive wild man.

- Meanwhile, Entwistle had a reputation as the quiet one but was actually a dark and troubled individual. However, the one close friendship that did emerge over the years was the one between John and Keith. The other two were somewhat jealous of this connection. Pete says, "Roger and I got the impression that John and Keith did almost everything together, including having sex with girls." Roadie Richard Cole remembers, "We were passing through this little town when Moon said to me, 'Stop the car.' Entwistle knew exactly what was going on, but he wasn't about to divulge anything. Moon had gone to fetch weedkiller and sugar so they could make a bomb. Moon let the fuckingthing off in the Caledonian Hotel in Edinburgh andwe all got thrown out."

- *Tommy* was a huge success. However, it was a make-or-break album for the band. Pete was increasingly unhappy with their musical direction, feeling the band was growing too old for the kind of music they were playing. Their last single, "Dogs," was a commercial flop. The band was also unable to make money touring because their shows relied on the destruction of instruments and amplifiers, leading to costly tours. Inspired by the increasingly complex albums The Who's rivals like The Beatles and The Beach Boys were putting together, Pete was determined to go all the way and make a concept album. The other band members were surprised at the direction of the album. Keith said, "It was, at the time, very un-Who-like. A lot of the songs were soft. We never played like that." However, they were supportive of the new direction. It was one last gamble to gain the band respectability and longevity, and it worked. *Tommy* was a massive hit and elevated The Who to a new level of success.

- The Tommy tour has to rank as one of the most important and artistically successful tours of all time. Amongst its many highlights, two are among the most important moments in late '60s rock. They played Woodstock in support of the album. In addition, they recorded the date at the University of Leeds Refectory. The album they released, *Live at Leeds*, is widely considered one of the greatest live albums of all time. We believe it is the most fantastic live album of all time, but no one asked us.

CHAPTER 4:

LIVE AT LEEDS AND *WHO'S NEXT*

1. The initial plan was to release a live album out of
    materials recorded at Electric Ballroom, Philadelphia
    on October 19, and the London Coliseum show on
    December 16, 1969. What happened to those
    materials?

    a. The band put them aside and released them
        later
    b. They were filmed for a movie which never
        panned out
    c. Pete burned them
    d. Pete lost them

2. Why did the band choose to record their live album
    in the unglamorous industrial city of Leeds?

    a. They recorded several shows and that was the
        best
    b. Pete's family spent holidays in Leeds
    c. The band wanted to make a statement
    d. The hall at Leeds University had excellent
        acoustics

3. What is the capacity at the Refectory located at Leeds University?
   a. 2,000
   b. 6,000
   c. 12,000
   d. 15,000

4. True or False: Pete was very unhappy with the quality of the recording of Live at Leeds.

5. True or False: Pete hated the crowd at the Leeds show, and that fueled his playing on the album.

6. When introducing the fantastic version of "Young Man Blues," Pete says the author has been described as a "jazz-sage." What does Keith Moon yell in the background?
   a. "A flavored chicken!"
   b. "My favorite spice!"
   c. "A type of sauce!"
   d. "A boring dish!"

7. The band also recorded their show at Hull for a live album. However, they decided not to use any of the tapes because of which problem?
   a. You couldn't hear the vocals
   b. You couldn't hear the drums
   c. You couldn't hear the bass
   d. You couldn't hear the guitar

8. The album of that Hull show was released on November 19, 2012. What did they do about the problem mentioned in the previous question?
   a. They released it warts and all
   b. They re-recorded the sections later in the studio
   c. They used parts from other shows
   d. They used parts from *Live at Leeds*

9. When the band returned to Leeds University in 2006, the tickets were more expensive. How much more did they cost more than 25 years later?
   a. £37
   b. £137
   c. £237
   d. £337

10. The cover of the album *Who's Next* referenced which film of the period?
    a. *Easy Rider*
    b. *The Graduate*
    c. *2001: A Space Odyssey*
    d. *Breathless*

11. Which song off Who's Next was intended as the last song on Pete's aborted *Lifehouse* project?
    a. "Won't Get Fooled Again"
    b. "Bargain"
    c. "Baba O'Reily"
    d. "The Song is Over"

12. True or False: The Who's experience at Woodstock inspired the song "Baba O'Reily."

13. True or False: Pete hated Glyn Johns' work producing *Who's Next.*

14. "Baba O'Reily" included a wonderful violin part played by Dave Arbus. How did the band play that part when performing the aforementioned song?
    a. Pete played a guitar solo
    b. They didn't play the part
    c. They hired a violinist
    d. Roger played it on the harmonica

15. "Behind Blue Eyes" is a particularly emotionally powerful song. What experience inspired Pete to write it?
    a. Overcoming sexual temptation
    b. Overcoming alcoholic dependence
    c. Overcoming drug dependence
    d. Overcoming sexual abuse

16. The ambitious *Lifehouse* project, which was the basis of *Who's Next,* never came to fruition. However, its plot foresaw a major technological innovation. What future development did Pete predict?
    a. Social media
    b. The internet
    c. Cellphones
    d. Netflix

17. Where was the epic "Won't Get Fooled Again" recorded?
    a. The Record Plant
    b. Stargroves
    c. Olympic Studios
    d. Sunset Studios

18. "My Wife" is probably the best received of John Entwistle's songs. However, he was not happy with the version on *Who's Next*. What did he feel was wrong with it?
    a. His bass
    b. It didn't rock hard
    c. The singing
    d. It didn't swing

19. True or False: Critics at the time did not recognize the brilliance of the album.

20. Where did Rolling Stone magazine rank the album in their original Top 500 Albums of All Time list?
    a. 30-40th place
    b. 20-29th place
    c. 10-19th place
    d. 1-9th place

ANSWERS

1. C. Pete burned them. Or, at least that is his story. Pete says, "we thought that we would get the best material. When we got back, we had 80 hours of tape. I said, 'Fuck that, I'm not going to sit through 80 hours of live stuff'. Let's face it; you'd get brainwashed. So we just scrapped the lot. We put it all on a bonfire to stop bootlegging." However, some of those performances have popped up elsewhere. So he may have been exaggerating for dramatic effect.

2. C. The band wanted to make a statement. Manager Kit Lambert recalls, "In those days live albums were always 'Live at the Colosseum in Rome' or 'Live at the Palladium,' 'Hollywood Bowl,' etc. I said, 'live' isn't really like that. Touring is much seedier. So why didn't we think of 'Live at Grimsby' or 'Live at Mud-on-Sea.' I looked at the schedule and said, 'You're in Hull on Wednesday and Leeds on Thursday [sic], so it's going to be 'Live at Hull' or 'Live at Leeds.' Things didn't go too well at Hull, so it had to be Leeds."

3. A. 2,000. It remains a particularly small and intimate venue. However, all the greats played there: Jimi Hendrix, Pink Floyd, Led Zeppelin. In 2006, the band went back and performed there again.

4. True. "They did a terrible job on the recording, they fucked it up incredibly. They got crackles all through it, horrible crackles, but I'm just going to put it out anyway." The band famously had "Crackling Noises OK — Do Not Correct" written on the album. Keith disagreed and was very happy with the sound. He says, "We sat Bob Pridden at the control panel on stage and left him to get on with the balance. The Hull show was quite good, but the Leeds one was really good. Bob worked well that night, bless him!"

5. False. Pete was uncharacteristically enthusiastic about the audience and the show in general. Pete says, "It just happened to be a good show, and it just happened to be one of the greatest audiences we've ever played to in our whole career, just by chance. They were incredible and, though you can't hear a lot of shouting and screaming in the background [on the record] … they're crazy — you know, they're fantastic. And we played it in their hall. The sound is all right — it's a good atmosphere.'

6. A. "A flavored chicken!" The joking discourse between Keith and Pete was quite affectionate and successful and can be heard throughout the album, especially the extended version. For example, when Pete introduces Tommy as "Thomas, a pot opera," Moon taps his drums and declares, "Quiet, quiet, it's a bleedin' opera, innit!"

7. C. You couldn't hear the bass. The band was happy with their show and sat down to listen to the show's tapes in Hull and could not hear the bass. Happily, all was not lost. Audio engineer Bob Pridden says, "We wanted to use Hull as the live recording rather than Leeds, but when we listened to the playback, the bass was missing. The interesting thing is that we obviously didn't listen all the way through. It was only when I was doing my research for this album that I found some tracks with the bass playing loud and clear, and with John on top form!"

8. D. They used parts from *Live at Leeds*. One reviewer wrote that "the experience of listening to *Live at Hull* is a bit disconcerting. It is like meeting the twin brother of a friend that you did not know had a twin at all."

9. A. £37. The original tickets were only 57.5 pence.

10. C. *2001: A Space Odyssey*. To many, the obelisk at the center of the cover suggested the one at the center of the inscrutable science fiction movie. Photographer Ethan Russell was driving around with the band, looking for a site for an appropriate photograph, when he spotted the slab of concrete on an intersection in central England. "I was taking test Polaroids, and [when I] looked up," Russell says, "Pete had peed on it. I thought, 'Okay!' [and] took about eight shots." In the photo, it looks like

everyone in the band urinated on the obelisk. However, "except for Pete's, the 'urine' was water we poured on the concrete. They couldn't perform!" The cover was not the only one considered. One had a picture of a large-breasted woman and another, a picture of Keith Moon in lingerie and a wig holding a whip.

11. A. "Won't Get Fooled Again." After the main character was killed, the "universal chord" is sounded. The government and army are left behind, and the song represents the desperation of the moment. The brilliant piece is highly political and can be seen as a reply to the more extreme elements of the counter-culture movement. Pete describes it as a song "that screams defiance at those who feel any cause is better than no cause."

12. True. Or, possibly their experience at the Isle of Wight Festival later on. As you remember, Pete did not enjoy his time at the legendary "peace andlove" festival. He recalls "the absolute desolation of teenagers at Woodstock, where audience members were strung out on acid, and 20 people had brain damage. The irony was that some listeners took the song to be a teenage celebration: 'Teenage Wasteland, yes! We're all wasted!'"

13. False. The sound on the album is so rich and crisp that it met Pete's exacting standards. He says it was

"the first Who material in a long time to be properly recorded." Perhaps his most significant contribution was insisting that the band keep *Who's Next* to a single album. Pete wanted to make it a double album, which would likely have diluted the impact of the concise and perfect album.

14. D. Roger played it on the harmonica.

15. A. Overcoming sexual temptation. Pete was married and tried not to sleep with groupies but had almost succumbed. After a show in Denver. He says that he went back to his room and wrote the words, "If my fist clenches, crack it open ...".

16. C. The internet. The project included reference to the grid, an electronic form of communication connecting everyone electronically.

17. B. Stargroves. Rolling Stones singer Mick Jagger owned the estate. It is just one of many classic songs and albums recorded using the Rolling Stones Mobile Studio.

18. D. It didn't swing. Therefore, John re-recorded it for his solo album *Rigor Mortis Sets In*. He claims that it wasn't autobiographical. However, he would later say, "When I wrote it, I didn't know it would come true. I didn't know my wives would make it a fucking sequel either."

19. False. Many of the classic rock albums of the time were panned by reviewers when they came out and

later reappraised. However, there was something about the impact of *Who's Next* that was immediate and universal. The Village Voice called it "the best hard rock album in years." Even Rolling Stone, known for its reviews tearing about the best albums of all time, wrote that the album was, "Intelligently conceived, superbly performed, brilliantly produced, and sometimes even exciting." By their standards, that was a good review.

20. B. 20-29th place. It was No. 28, to be precise. We will try to ignore the updated list, which placed the masterpiece at No. 77.

DID YOU KNOW

- The Who had been known throughout their career as the ultimate live band. Therefore, it was a huge deal when it came time for them to release a live album. The result invented the live album concept as a separate and vital part of the band's recorded catalog. While other rock bands had released live albums, they featured arrangements similar to the original with studio overdubs. *Live at Leeds*, meanwhile, aimed to capture new and different arrangements of the songs in their raw and primal glory. It was one of the best shows by one of the best live bands in rock history, to top it off. Therefore, the blueprint the band set on *Live at Leeds*was often imitated but never bettered. As Pete says,"You can always feel what happens to an audiencewhen you move them. And at Leeds University it was the first time that we really had moved an audience, and you never forget that. Everything came together at once — the songs, the power of the band, the confidence of the band, the band's ability. Everything nearly came together all at once,but it still kept its rough edges. The Who were always dangerous. We never ever lost that and still haven't."

- The band was going for a huge and all-encompassing sound in *Live at Leeds*. They had just switched to a far bigger and more sophisticated amplification system. The guitar was coming out of four 4 x 12 cabinets topped with two 100 watt Hiwatt amplifiers. The PA system had an output of 2,000 watts and cost an estimated £5,000. Pete said around the time of the recording that "We are trying to sophisticate our sound a little to make it a little less ear rending. We haven't got any louder, but our PA has got bigger. It's now 1,500 watts, and it just chucks it out. That's what's deafening, people. One of our troubles is Keith Moon — he's just so deafening. If we do a two-and-a-half-hour show, he just starts playing like a machine."

- The follow-up to *Tommy* was not meant to be a regular album. Instead, Pete planned a rock opera that would be far more grandiose than its predecessor, which he called *Lifehouse*. The inspiration was the almost religious experiences he had in some of the performances of *Tommy*. "I've seen moments in Who gigs where the vibrations were becoming so pure that I thought the whole world was just going to stop, the whole thing was just becoming so unified." The plot Pete had in mind was "a kinda futuristic scene … It's a fantasy set at a time when rock 'n roll didn't exist. The world was completely collapsing, and the only experience that anybody ever had was through test tubes. In a way, they lived as if they were in television programs. Everything was programmed. The enemies were people who gave us entertainment intravenously, and the heroes were savages who'd kept rock 'n roll as a primitive force and had gone to live with it in the woods. The story was about these two sides coming together and having a brief battle."

- As part of the project, Pete intended to write music that would reflect the crowd's personality. "Everybody would be snapped out of their programmed environment through this rock and roll-induced liberated selflessness. The lifehouse was where the music was played, and where the young people would collect to discover rock music as a powerful catalyst — a religion as it were. Then I began to feel 'Well, why just simulate it? Why not try and make it happen?" To make this happen, Pete wanted to gather a regular crowd at the Vic Theatre and compile information on all of them. It would include an astrological chart, their hobbies, and each person's physical appearance. The characteristics would then be fed into a computer with songs for each individual and one musical note, leading to mass nirvana.

- Not surprisingly, the concept proved too complex and elusive. Pete found himself unable to explain what he wanted to the other people involved. He had a nervous breakdown as a result. Pete says, "the fatal flaw ... was getting obsessed with trying to make a fantasy a reality rather than letting the film speak for itself." However, despite the difficulties he faced with the project, Pete kept turning back to it over and over. Elements of it would feature in the *Who Are You* album. In 1999, the most complete version of the *Lifehouse* storylineappeared in a radio play that Pete wrote. That year,he also released a box set he called *The Lifehouse Chronicles*, which includes all of the variations on the concept, including the radio play. Pete even wrote a play about his experiences trying to finish *Lifehouse*, which he named *Psychoderelict*. As of 2021,a graphic novel of *Lifehouse* is due out at some pointin the future. It is fair to say that the project has haunted him his entire life.

CHAPTER 5:

QUADROPHENIA

1. Right before the release of *Quadrophenia*, the band released "Join Together." Though now considered a classic, Daltrey disliked it at the time. Why?
   a. The lyrics
   b. The chorus
   c. His singing
   d. The synthesizer

2. *Relay*, released on November 25, 1972, was the second non-album single The Who put out for a long time. How many years later did they put out the next one?
   a. 12 years
   b. 22 years
   c. 32 years
   d. 44 years

3. Which Marvin Gaye song did The Who use as the B-side for "Join Together?"

a. "Baby Don't You Do It"
b. "One More Heartache"
c. "Your Precious Love"
d. "You're All I Need to Get By"

4. How many songs on *Quadrophenia* were written by John Entwistle?
    a. 0
    b. 1
    c. 2
    d. 3

5. Each of the four sides of the *Quadrophenia* represents one of the members of the band. Which member was the "Is It Me?" side (side two of the first record) dedicated to?
    a. Pete
    b. Keith
    c. John
    d. Roger

6. The song "I'm the One" is about being a member of a gang. It was written about the true experiences of one of the band members. Which member was it?
    a. Roger
    b. Pete
    c. John
    d. Keith

7. The band recorded the early sessions for *Quadrophenia* in a mobile studio owned by a member of The Faces. Which member was it?
    a. Rod Stewart
    b. Ronnie Lane
    c. Ian McLagan
    d. Kenney Jones

8. True or False: John thought that *Quadrophenia* was a pretentious mess.

9. Following the album's release, the band parted ways with their long-time managerial team of Kit Lambert and Chris Stamp. What was the cause of the split?
    a. Creative differences
    b. The band was frustrated they weren't bigger
    c. Personal differences
    d. Financial differences

10. "Love Reign O'er Me" is a beautiful song. Which mainstream music star was so impressed that they asked Pete if he actually wrote it?
    a. Frank Sinatra
    b. Diana Ross
    c. Barbara Streisand
    d. Karen Carpenter

11. True or False: Due to all the praise Roger received for his exceptional vocal performance on the album, he was delighted with his vocals.

12. True or False: Pete and Roger didn't talk to each other for months due to the violence and mutual strife they experienced while recording *Quadrophenia*.

13. Like many The Who albums, *Quadrophenia* only reached No. 2 in the UK and US charts. What album kept it out of first on the Billboard charts?
    a. *Goats Head Soup* - The Rolling Stones
    b. *Brothers and Sisters* - The Allman Brothers Band
    c. *Goodbye Yellow Brick Road* - Elton John
    d. *Inner Visions* - Stevie Wonder

14. Which political event had an impact on *Quadrophenia*'s album sales?
    a. The Watergate Trials
    b. The Vietnam War
    c. The occupation of Wounded Knee
    d. The OPEC oil embargo

15. True or False: *Rolling Stone* magazine panned the album for being too pretentious.

16. Tensions between Pete and Roger beset the *Quadrophenia* tour. What was the cause of them?
    a. Alcohol
    b. Drugs
    c. Sex
    d. Keyboards

17. The band often destroyed a good amount of equipment on tour and at their hotels. However, on

one date of the *Quadrophenia* tour, the Royal Canadian Mounted Police arrested The Who. Where did this happen?
   a. Toronto
   b. Ottawa
   c. Vancouver
   d. Montreal

18. In one of the shows on the tour, Keith passed out. What happened next?
    a. The show was canceled
    b. The drummer from the warm-up band filled in
    c. Roger played the drums
    d. A fan played the drums

19. The Who launched a retrospective *Quadrophenia* tour. In what year did they do so?
    a. 2011
    b. 2012
    c. 2013
    d. 2014

20. Which Seattle grunge icon was obsessed with "Love, Reign O'er" Me?
    a. Kurt Cobain
    b. Eddie Vedder
    c. Chris Cornell
    d. Layne Staley

ANSWERS

1. D. The synthesizer. Although it did not play a significant part in the song's arrangement, it annoyed Roger. "At the time, I was still very doubtful about bringing in the synthesizer. I felt that, with a lot of songs, we'd end up spending so much time creating these piddly one-note noises that it would've been better just doing it on guitar. I mean, I'm a guitar man. I love the guitar; to me, it's the perfect rock instrument. I don't think Pete did much with those sequencing things that he couldn't have done on his guitar anyway."

2. C. 32 years. The next one was Real Good Looking Boy, released in 2004.

3. A. "Baby Don't You Do It." The Who had previously played it in 1964-1965, and it was a favorite of Roger's.

4. A. 0. Most of the band's albums were dominated by Pete, but *Quadrophenia* was the Pete Townshend show. It was the first album wherein every song was written by the guitarist.

5. C. John. By dedicating each side to another member of the band, Pete hoped to reflect how the different personalities in the band complemented and

tormented each other. The sides were: "Bell Boy" (Keith), "Is It Me?" (John), "Helpless Dancer" (Roger), and "Love Reign O'er Me" (Pete).

6. B. Pete. Although Roger had been in a gang for far longer, Pete had some experience as well. He recalls, "As a young man, I needed, and wanted, to be part of a gang of young men. I'd grown up in a gang, one that started when I was a street kid in Acton when I was four years old, running wild when it was still safe to do so. What happens when you're subsumed in a gang or collective of any kind is that you soon find the parts of you that don't fit, that can't be accommodated. For Jimmy — for all the piss-taking I got from the band about following the Indian spiritual master Meher Baba — what didn't fit the mod gang he was in was his spiritual confusion, his lack of a sense of deep human purpose."

7. B. Ronnie Lane. The sessions were incredibly successful, to the surprise of everyone in the band. Even Pete gushed about it. He says: "The other guys in the band hadn't had to do very much,creatively speaking, to make that happen — just support me during recording, and then do the roadwork to back it up. I felt supported by the other guys, especially at the moment they first started to play my new stuff. Running through one of the first songs we recorded for *Quadrophenia*, I remember thinking that we'd never sounded better, or played

with such conviction on unproved material. This was especially true of Roger. He sang like a raging bear. His "Love Reign O'er Me" will never be surpassed."

8. False. While John notably didn't like the *Lifehouse* idea, he seemed to connect with *Quadrophenia*. His bass playing on the album is phenomenal, arguably the best on any of the band's studio albums. Pete calls John's contribution "Stunning, he was also wonderful to work with — meticulous, disciplined, funny, and inspired. I loved it that he wrote out his brass parts on music manuscript paper like a proper composer. What he arranged and played on a whole variety of exotic brass instruments fit my own synthesizer and string arrangements perfectly."

9. D. Financial differences. Roger did an audit of the band's finances and found that things did not line up correctly. Stamp and Lambert insist that the singer was bitter because they rejected his solo album. Unfortunately, Kit had also developed a severe drug problem. It was a difficult decision for Pete, who was very close to the duo. "My strategy was always to run to Kit Lambert or Chris Stamp to fly new ideas. By 1973, they had both lost interest in The Who to some extent. Kit had long since left the stage as my songwriting mentor, but I was hoping he would co-produce. He turned out to be too distracted."

10. C. Barbara Streisand. Pete wasn't offended. "Barbra Streisand touched my cheek during the Kennedy Center Awards show [in 2008, where soul singer Bettye LaVette sang the tune] and asked me if I had 'really written that song? It's beautiful.' Nice moment for me."

11. False. Author Richard Barnes says that Roger even delayed the release because "Roger used to complain that his voice had got lost in the mix. It was a bit of a dense, heavy mix, like an assault on the senses." If there was a problem, they certainly fixed it. Roger sounds great.

12. False. Though Pete and Roger had exchanged harsh words and serious blows, they did not hold it against each other. Pete says, "Roger punched me once, and I'm sure I asked for it. And he could have killed me, he had a hell of a punch. Luckily, I just lost my memory for an hour or two. He was very sweet afterward. Roger and I have had our spats, but he is really a good and loving man. I knew that then and I'm more aware of it now. But we were both under incredible strain. I'd arrived for a rehearsal four hours late, after preparing stage tapes. It's all ancient history."

13. C. "Goodbye Yellow Brick Road" - Elton John. All of these albums were on the charts around that time. As you can see, October 1973 was quite a month for music.

14. D. The OPEC oil embargo. Because vinyl is a byproduct of petrol, there was an actual vinyl challenge. Therefore, many fans had to wait to obtain their copies.

15. False. *Rolling Stone* again gave it a relatively good review. Reviewer Lenny Kaye wrote that it is "a beautifully performed and magnificently recorded essay of a British youth mentality in which [The Who] played no little part," adding that, "it might easily be said that The Who as a whole have never sounded better." However, he was not convinced by the writing, and therefore Kaye concluded that "on its own terms, *Quadrophenia* falls short of the mark."

16. D. Keyboards. Keith wanted to hire a keyboard player for the tour. However, Roger insisted that the band remain a four-piece. Therefore, they had to use tapes for the keyboard parts. Unfortunately, they continuously malfunctioned. As a result of these problems, Roger punched Pete. In another incident, Pete forced sound man Bob Pridden on stage and yelled and humiliated him. He then kicked over amps and destroyed the tapes. It was one of the worst tours the band ever had.

17. D. Montreal. After they trashed their hotel, the police were called, and 14 individuals were arrested. Keith Moon reportedly complained to authorities that his

jail cell was too small since "I believe I booked a suite." Management ended up paying $6,000 in damages, and the band was released.

18. D. A fan played the drums. Keith had taken horse tranquilizers and washed them down with brandy. (Yes, horse tranquilizers.) Moon played pretty badly for a few songs. However, when they hit "Won't Get Fooled Again," he passed out. He woke up for "Magic Bus" … and passed out again. The drummer for warm-up band Lynyrd Skynyrd, Artemus Pyle, was there, but he wouldn't go on because he didn't know the songs. Therefore, Pete asked, "Is there anybody out there who can play drums?" 19-year-old Scot Halpin of Muscatine, Iowa, volunteered.

19. B. 2012. That year the band launched a 36-date tour to commemorate the album.

20. B. Eddie Vedder. The Pearl Jam singer credits the song with saving his life. It saved my life," the singer said. "It was something I could catch because for some reason it seemed like I could not relate to anyone in the world. With no one in my school and certainly with no one in my house, and all of a sudden, this London guy named Pete came in who knew everything that was going on in my life." As he wrote later, The Who was Eddie's favorite band. "I was around nine when a babysitter snuck *Who's*

Next onto the turntable," he wrote. "The parents were gone. The windows shook. The shelves were rattling. Rock 'n roll. That began an exploration into music that had soul, rebellion, aggression, affection. Destruction. And this was all Who music. Imagine, as a kid, stumbling upon the locomotive that is *Live at Leeds*. 'Hi, my name is Eddie. I'm 10 years old and I'm getting my fucking mind blown!' Pearl Jam often plays "Love, Reign O'er Me" live, and Eddie has played with The Who several times.

DID YOU KNOW

- There was intense pressure on Pete to repeat the success of *Tommy*, not just in terms of its commercial success but also the artistic scope of the piece. He was also highly concerned that the band was starting to drift apart. "We were all bored with playing *Tommy* and only played three songs from *Who's Next* on stage. I wanted a *Tommy* replacement for our stage act. And the guys in the band were itchy, I think. I was looking for a way to stroke the four eccentric egos of the guys in the band. We'd always been different, but by 1972, I felt I'd one last chance to do something that might hold us together and unify us in the eyes of our fans." After the failure of *Lifehouse*, Pete decided to pursue a more digestible and attainable project to achieve these goals. "In this case, the four members of The Who. So it was the reverse of what I was pitching in the music papers. In 1972/73 there were no mods, no 'armies' or 'uniforms' of any kind in the pop-rock audience, just big shirts with big collars, and haircuts from a Shakespeare play. Part of what I wanted to do was re-establish with our fans the principles they themselves had set up when we'd started. I think The Who had been servants of the audience in 1964-65, not the other way around. Our job was always to give our audience something they needed, not make them think we were stars. Inside The Who, Keith Moon was not just doing a 'star' thing but taking it to extremes. He was behaving like a Saudi Prince. We all had our part toplay. We'd lost perspective partly because our stageshows were so fucking intense. We felt inviolable …I think I felt a kinship with teenaged fans, but by 1972, I was 27 years old and maybe this was a last grab at writing my follow-up to *Tommy*; my *Catcherin the Rye*."

- Tensions between Roger and Pete were sometimes incredibly high and erupted into violence. After the band had completed *Quadrophenia*, they went to make a film to promote the album. However, Roger had no interest in participating and told Pete. The guitarist was drunk out of his mind and assaulted the singer. As Roger remembers, "Pete, fueled by the best part of a bottle of brandy, went off like a firecracker." At that moment, Pete hurled a guitar at Roger. The singer recalled, "it whistled past my ear and glanced off my shoulder, very nearly bringing a much earlier end to The Who. I replied with an uppercut to the jaw." It knocked Townshend to the ground, where he cracked his head. I thought I'd killed him." Dqaltrey accompanied Pete to the hospital, holding his hand the whole way.

- The recording and touring experience behind *Quadrophenia* had left the band, and Pete in particular, exhausted and demoralized. Despite getting some good reviews, the album did not get the respect it deserved. Friend of the band Richard Barnes says of the album, "It's like a solo Townshend project. *Quadrophenia* works because it's just a wonderful piece of art, the power of the music is immense. But in many ways, *Quadrophenia* was a failure. It was a critical success and it sold a lot, but it was one of those albums that was worthy. Everyone had it in their collection, but didn't play it much." None of the singles from the album did well in the charts, and few people say it is their favorite The Who album. Pete summed it up unkindly at the time, "The whole thing was a disaster." The guitarist later explained why he was unhappy with it. "I've always liked it and been proud of it, but it failed to provide The Who with an alternative 70-minute rock opera stage act to replace *Tommy*. I only started working on it to achieve that, so I was unwilling to talk about it for a long time. It was there as an album if anyone wanted to hear it, but the big picture had never happened."

- However, in later years, the album has found renewed and well-deserved respect. Today, it is considered to be in the higher echelons of the band's back catalog, and Pete is justifiably proud of it. The Who reprised the album later on a live tour. In a beautiful symmetry, Roger was the producer of the entire event. The two had fought ferociously while the album was recorded. However, they had learned to cooperate and appreciate all they had achieved together. Pete was touched. "I loved it. I suppose there was a bit of me that enjoyed it because it was such a grand celebration of the music in such a fabulous venue. Roger had total control of that show. He had demanded it when I asked him to perform it with me. I thought he did afantastic job as a director."

CHAPTER 6

THE WHO BY NUMBERS

1. By all accounts, the recording of the album *The Who By Numbers* saw the band at its most dysfunctional. Which member proved the reliable one at this challenging time for the band?
    a. Roger
    b. Pete
    c. John
    d. Keith

2. In the mid-'70s Keith moved from London to another happening city. Which town did he relocate to?
    a. New York
    b. Paris
    c. Los Angeles
    d. Rome

3. Which band member designed the cover of *The Who By Numbers*?

a. Roger
b. Pete
c. John
d. Keith

4. Which song on *The Who By Numbers* was described by Pete as "me wanting to kill myself."
    a. "Blue, Red, and Grey"
    b. "However Much I Booze"
    c. "How Many Friends"
    d. "Dreaming From the Waist"

5. On May 31, 1976, the band set a record for the world's loudest band. How loud were they playing at the time?
    a. 106 decibels
    b. 116 decibels
    c. 126 decibels
    d. 136 decibels

6. True or False: John hated *The Who By Numbers* and thought it was the worst album they ever made.

7. True or False: "Squeeze Box" ended up as a big hit. However, Pete intended it as a joke and disliked the song.

8. True or False: The Sex Pistols respected The Who, even though they detested the other British bands of the era, such as Pink Floyd, Led Zeppelin, and The Rolling Stones?

9. The song "Slip Kid" was initially intended for another The Who project. What project was it slated for?
    a. *Tommy*
    b. *Lifehouse*
    c. *The Who Sells Out*
    d. *Quadrophenia*

10. Which song off of *Who Are You* does Pete most hate to play?
    a. "New Song"
    b. "Who Are You"
    c. "Guitar and Pen"
    d. "Sister Disco"

11. Which of these music superstars *didn't* appear in the *Tommy* film?
    a. Tina Turner
    b. Stevie Wonder
    c. Eric Clapton
    d. Elton John

12. True or False: The *Tommy* film won the main competition at the Cannes Film Festival.

13. True or False: *Tommy* director Ken Russell did not like the band or their music.

14. Which member of the cast of the *Tommy* film ended up in the hospital during filming?

a. Ann-Margret
b. Oliver Reed
c. Roger Daltrey
d. Jack Nicholson

15. The years of the events in *Tommy* were changed from the album to the movie. What was the song 1921 called in the film?
    a. "1931"
    b. "1941"
    c. "1951"
    d. "1961"

16. True or False: Jack Nicholson played a relatively minor part in the film. He agreed because he was a massive fan of the band.

17. The Who released a rarities album called *Odds & Sods* in 1974. On the album, they are wearing gear associated with which sport?
    a. Football
    b. Soccer
    c. Cricket
    d. Rugby

18. Which member of the band compiled the tracks that would appear on the *Odds & Sods* album?
    a. Roger
    b. Pete
    c. John
    d. Keith

19. The Who anthem "Long Live Rock" did not appear on any albums before *Odds & Sods*. In what year did the band record it?
    a. 1968
    b. 1970
    c. 1972
    d. 1974

20. The song "The Naked Eye" had appeared in the band's live repertoire for years before they finally released it in *Odds & Sods*. Why wasn't it released before?
    a. It didn't fit the album's themes
    b. The band didn't like the song
    c. The record company didn't like it
    d. They had trouble recording a good version

ANSWERS

1. C. John. Pete remembers that "I felt partly responsible because The Who's recording schedule had, as usual, dragged on and on, sweeping all individuals and their needs aside. Glyn worked harder on *The Who by Numbers* than I've ever seen him. He had to, not because the tracks were weak or the music poor, but because the group was so useless. We played cricket between takes or went to the pub. I personally had never done that before. I felt detached from my own songs, from the whole record. Recording the album seemed to take me nowhere. Roger was angry with the world at the time. Keith seemed as impetuous as ever, on the wagon one minute, off the next. John was obviously gathering strength throughout the whole period; the great thing about it was he seemed to know we were going to need him more than ever before in the coming year."

2. C. Los Angeles. Hollywood, to be precise. The band was concerned that he was getting lost over there. Pete recalls that he used to have a conversation with Roger about "where music was going to go — particularly in this country — and whether we should be involved in it, and the problem with [drummer Keith Moon] living in America and

living that Hollywood lifestyle and whether we should try and force him to come back to England ... all those kind of things."

3. C. John. It was his first (but not his last) art piece. He says, "The first [piece of artwork] release[d] is *The Who By Numbers* cover, which I never got paid for, so now I'm going to get paid. (laughs) We were taking it in turns to do the covers. It was Pete's turn before me, and we did the *Quadrophenia* cover, which cost about the same as a small house back then, about £16,000. My cover cost £32."

4. A. "Blue, Red, and Grey." He remembers that "Glyn Johns wanted it on the album. I cringed when he picked it. He heard it on a cassette and said, 'What's that?' I said, 'Nothing.' He said, 'No. Play it.' I said, 'Really, it's nothing. Just me playing ukulele.' But he insisted on doing it. I said, 'What? That fucking thing? Here's me wanting to commit suicide, and you're going to put that thing on the record?" However, Pete says that the misery on the album should not be taken too literally. "I certainly didn't feel a lack of friendship, and I certainly didn't feel suicidal. I think I may have been a bit angry occasionally."

5. C. 126 Decibels. The sound of a motorcycle engine is about 90 decibels. Incidentally, noise above 120 decibels can cause immediate and irreparable

damage to your ears. It is not too surprising that all members of the band have suffered hearing loss.

6. False. John seems to have been reasonably pleased with it: "The best we've done since the last one. I like the cover. That's pretty good."

7. True. In the liner notes of the remastered version, Pete wrote that the song was "Intended as a poorly aimed dirty joke. I had bought myself an accordion and learned to play it one afternoon. The polka-esque rhythm I managed to produce from it brought forth this song. Amazingly recorded by The Who to my disbelief. Further incredulity was caused when it became a hit for us in the USA." However, Roger loved it. "It's so refreshingly simple. An incredibly catchy song. It doesn't pretend to be anything other than what it is, and I love it for that."

8. True. The Sex Pistols used to cover "Substitute" and admired The Who and their uncompromising music and destructive shows.

9. B. *Lifehouse*. Thankfully, Pete resurrected it for *The Who By Numbers*. He considers it one of his best "'Slip Kid' came across as a warning to young kids getting into music that it would hurt them — It was almost parental in its assumed wisdom." But it remains relevant today: "You could put it into the voice of some young Islamic student who decides

to go fight in Syria and ends up in ISIS being forced to chop people's heads off, and it would fit."

10. D. "Sister Disco." The reason? Roger likes to sing it. When asked which song he hated playing, Petesays, "I think actually 'Sister Disco' qualifies, yeah 'Sister Disco' I hate even more than 'Dreaming From the Waist' because there is a point in which every time we've done it where Roger comes over to me, stands next to me and makes some kind of sappy smile, which is supposed to communicate some kind of Everly Brothers relationship we havefor the audience, which isn't there. It's supposed tobe an act where I'm supposed to collude like, 'We know each other very well. We look like enemies but we are friends really,' kind of look. Often, that will be the moment where I look him in the face and go 'you fucking wanker' and he gets angry when I do that." They have a somewhat complex relationship.

11. C. Stevie Wonder. Pete remembers, "Elton was already stupidly rich, arriving in a massive Rolls Royce like the queen's and with his own number plate. He is always a joy to work with. Eric was fresh from heroin addiction, just drinking beer and chasing after Ann-Margret even though her husband and manager were always by her side."

12. False. The movie was shown at the prestigious festival but was not entered into the competition. The film got a standing ovation.

13. True. However, he was very attracted to the script and put a memorable imprint on the movie. Pete remembers, "Ken was bombastic, energetic, funny, tireless, and inspiring. He had an obsessive eye for detail and planning that I now realize every great film director needs or in its place the absolute certainty that they can accept what happens when it happens and adapt to it. I never had a bad moment with Ken. During the *Tommy* film, he only ever slept for about four hours."

14. A. Ann-Margaret. But she took it like a champ. The actress remembers, "It was such fun! They had built a wooden tube coming from way above to pour the things down to make it shoot out at me. No one had tried it before. Ken wanted me to look up and pretend that I don't see anything until it hits me. And when the beans hit me, it just THREW me. My goodness! When I threw the champagne bottle at the TV set, it really smashed. They got rid of all the broken glass on the carpet, but they had not gotten rid of all the jagged glass in the TV set. And Ken wanted me to thrash my arms around. And of course, one time, I brought my hands up, and the soap suds were pink from blood. So they took me away, put loads of towels on me. And here I come

into the hospital, looking like a drowned person in this silver-knit shrinking catsuit with blood all over. There were 27 stitches. I've never done a movie like that before or since. But the whole experience was wonderful."

15. C. 1951. The film was changed to make it more contemporary. The war in which Tommy's father disappeared was World War I rather than World War II. The new dates allowed them to bring the later events into the current day and thus include direct commentary on the culture of the '60s and '70s. Other than that, the plot was not changed much. Ken Russell said, "This in no way deviated from his [Townshend's] original but plugged in the gaps where I found the story obscure or just non-existent."

16. False. Jack was fascinated with director KenRussell. Jack said, "I'd like to work with anyone whose work seems to me to have some validity in its own terms, and that has to be true of anyone who can survive long enough in this business to beregarded as an old hand. That's why I want to workwith Ken Russell, though I'll only be doing a few days on Tommy as the Doctor. Russell's films intrigue me, some I like very much, some I don't like at all, and I want to find out what makes him tick."

17. A. Football. They can be seen wearing football helmets spelling out the word rock.

18. C. John. Somewhat alienated from the process of making the *Tommy* movie, John was given the job of finding the best tracks the band had never released. He says, "I tried to arrange it like a parallel sort of Who career — what singles we might have released and what album tracks we might have released. It could have been a double album, there was that much material."

19. 1972. However, Pete wrote it in 1971. It was intended for inclusion in the aborted *Lifehouse* project. The song plays a vital role in Pete's conceptual development. As he explained, "Well, there are dozens of these self-conscious hymns to the last fifteen years appearing now, and here's another one. This was featured briefly in the film for which Keith made his acting debut, *That'll Be The Day*. Billy Fury sang it. This is most definitely the definitive version. I had an idea once for a new album about the history of The Who called *Rock Is Dead — Long Live Rock!* That idea later blossomed into *Quadrophenia*."

20. D. They had trouble recording a good version. Or at least that is what Pete thought. "This number was written around a riff that we often played on stage at the end of our act around the time we were touring early *Tommy*. It came to be one of our best

stage numbers, this was never released because we always hoped we would get a good live version one day. But then we're such a lousy live group." If you say so, Pete.

DID YOU KNOW?

- *The Who By Numbers* was written at a miserable time for Pete. He turned 30 in May 1975 and was undergoing an existential crisis. The guitarist experienced the worst writer's block of his career. He says, "[The songs] were written with me stoned out of my brain in my living room, crying my eyes out ... detached from my own work and the whole project t... I felt empty." Roger says he regrets not reaching out to Pete more at the time. "

- "*The Who By Numbers* is very dark because Pete was going through some terrible agonies, but I didn't realize this at the time. We thought, if he wants space, we'll give him some space — when what we should have done was been there saying, 'You all right, Pete?' But that's just the way he was and still is. There's a side to him that is like a stone wall, and what he really wants you to do is knock down the fucking wall and come through it, which takes a lot of effort all the time. I understand it now, but I didn't understand it then. So it led to this brooding, deep, introspective album. He was boozing a lot, and I think he was having problems with his marriage, trying to balance that family life with rock 'n roll, 'cause they don't balance. But I love that album."

- Feeling he had very little left to give, Pete wondered if it was time for the band to break up. "Before the emergence of punk, The Who was the only band that actually sat around a table to decide 'Should we go on or not?' Would we be doing music a favor if we just fucking stopped? We considered that." That is one of the reasons the band engaged in making movies and large concept albums. They were not sure of the direction of their music.

- Roger was thrilled to put concept albums behind him after the release of *Quadrophenia*. He found them pretentious and did not understand why the fans seemed to prefer the rock operas to the regular albums. "Nobody wanted to listen to what [else] we were doing. *Who's Next* holds up much better, but nobody wanted to take it seriously because it was just nine songs and no great thing about a bloody spastic."

- The *Tommy* movie is a strange film, and the band had plenty of doubts about the direction Ken Russell was taking it in. However, it is without a doubt a commercial and critical success. It earned $27 million in the US and many millions more worldwide. *The New York Times* review captures the magic of the movie. It really shouldn't work. But somehow, it does. "It may be the most overproduced movie ever made, but there is wit and reason for this. It is the last word in pop art ... Everything, including the sound level, is too much. But even this works in an odd way. The victim of the movie is as much the person sitting in the audience as it is Tommy." *Variety* was filled with praise "The production is magnificent, the multitrack sound (tradenamed Quintophonic) terrific, the casting and acting great, and the name cameos most showmanly." However, there were skeptics. The famed Gene Siskel wrote "a disappointing, slap-dash pictorialization of the fine music of The Who [with] no cinematic flow." Hey, at least he likes the music!

CHAPTER 7

WHO ARE YOU AND THE DEATH OF KEITH MOON

1. Tragically, the cover of the album has a sign foreshadowing the imminent death of Keith Moon. Where does it appear?
   a. On a chair
   b. On a bus
   c. On an amplifier
   d. On Keith's chest

2. Which habit of Pete's caused delays in the recording of *Who Are You*?
   a. His drinking
   b. Sleeping in
   c. Spending time with his kids
   d. Car racing

3. The song "Who Are You" is written about a crazy night of drinking Pete had with members of another band. Which band got soused with him?

    a. The Clash
    b. The Sex Pistols
    c. The Damned
    d. The Misfits

4. True or False: *Rolling Stone* magazine panned "Who Are You" as one of the worst albums by the band.

5. Roger was so upset with Glyn John's production of one of the songs on *Who Are You* that he punched the legendary producer. Which song inspired this bout of unnecessary violence?
    a. "New Song"
    b. "Had Enough"
    c. "Sister Disco"
    d. "Music Must Change"

6. One of the songs on the album was played in a 6/8 rhythm. Keith, in his terrible state, was unable to play the tricky rhythm. Which song did the drummer have difficulty with?
    a. "Sister Disco"
    b. "Who Are You"
    c. "Trick of the Light"
    d. "The Music Must Change"

7. What is the song "Sister Disco" about?
    a. It is a defense of disco music
    b. It is an attack on disco music
    c. It is not about disco music
    d. No one knows

8. As often happened with The Who albums, *Who Are You* reached No. 2 in the Billboard charts. Which album kept it off the top spot?
    a. *Rumors* - Fleetwood Mac
    b. *Saturday Night Fever* - Bee Gees
    c. *Boston* - Don't Look Back
    d. *Grease* - Original Soundtrack

9. The documentary *The Kids Are Alright* about the band came out in 1979. It included footage of the band on tour. How did the wives of the band members react when they saw the raw footage?
    a. One of them filed for divorce
    b. They tried to stop the movie from being released
    c. They loved it
    d. They offered to work for the director

10. The movie, *The Kids Are Alright,* opens with a spectacular TV performance, ending in an orgy of destruction. What show were they on?
    a. The Smothers Brothers Comedy Hour
    b. The Lawrence Welk Show
    c. The Tonight Show Starring Johnny Carson
    d. The Dean Martin Show

11. *The Kids Are Alright* features some excellent live performances. Which of the following songs on the soundtrack was performed at Woodstock?

a. "Young Man Blues"
b. "Anyway, Anyhow, Anywhere"
c. "Pinball Wizard"
d. "My Generation"

12. The version of "A Quick One While He's Away" on *The Kids Are Alright* was long thought to have been lost. Where did they perform it?
    a. The Rolling Stones Rock and Roll Circus
    b. The Monterey Pop Festival
    c. American Bandstand
    d. Beat-Club

13. The TV show *CSI* regularly uses The Who songs as theme songs for its various releases. What was the name of the show that featured the song "Who Are You" in the opening credits?
    a. *CSI: Crime Scene Investigation*
    b. *CSI: Miami*
    c. *CSI: Cyber*
    d. *CSI: NY*

14. Keith released his only solo album, *Two Sides of The Moon*, in March 1975. How many guest musicians featured on the album?
    a. 30
    b. 40
    c. 50
    d. 60

15. True or False: Keith Moon and John Lennon lived together in a beach house in Santa Monica and became best friends.

16. On the night of Keith's death, he attended the premiere of a movie. Which movie was it?
    a. *Sgt. Peppers Lonely Hearts Club Band*
    b. *The Buddy Holly Story*
    c. *Grease*
    d. *Midnight Express*

17. Another musician had died in the same apartment Keith Moon spent his last night. Which musician was it?
    a. Brian Jones
    b. Paul Kossoff
    c. Mama Cass
    d. Jim Morrison

18. True or False: Not long before Keith died, Pete told him he had to improve his playing or be fired from The Who.

19. True or False. Keith once injured a hotel staff member by locking him in the bathroom as he used explosives to blow up a toilet.

20. When Rolling Stone Magazine did its best drummer of all-time list, where did Keith rank?
    a. No.1
    b. No.2

c. No.3
d. No.4

97

ANSWERS

1. A. On a chair. Keith is sitting on a backward-facing chair. On its backrest are the chilling words, "Not to Be Taken Away." They refer to the chair, of course. He sat there to hide his distended stomach, which was the result of years of alcohol abuse.

2. C. Spending time with his kids. Pete was focused on being a good family man. He would pick up hiskids every day from school in the afternoon. Unfortunately, Roger is not a morning person and likes to work in the afternoon. So the timing of the sessions was problematic.

3. B. The Sex Pistols. Pete wrote Who Are You about meeting Steve Jones and Paul Cook of the Sex Pistols after an awful thirteen-hour encounter with Allen Klein [former Beatles manager]. Pete explained, "we socialized a few times. Got drunk (well, I did) and I have to say to their credit, for a couple of figurehead anarchists, they seemed sincerely concerned about my decaying condition at the time."

4. True. The original review complained that "The drive we expect from The Who is replaced by chunky, sometimes clunky orchestration — strings, horns, synthesizer music. This gives one the feeling

that The Who isn't moving, that they aren't gearing up for a great rock and roll shoot-out with the competition, heading off for better times, claiming the future — rather, they're face-to-face with limbo, and trying to think their way out of it."

5. B. "Had Enough." Roger remembers, "I had a punch-up with Glyn Johns, mainly because he put strings on John's track 'Had Enough.' I went into the studio in the afternoon the day before they put on the strings. I thought, 'fucking hell, strings on a Who track?' When I heard it, it was just slushy strings, and I don't like slushy strings." Glyn quit, and who can blame him. No pun intended.

6. D. "The Music Must Change." Therefore, there were no drums on the track, just footsteps, and some cymbals. John remembered Keith "couldn't think of anything to play." On another occasion, co-producer Astley recalls, "I was doing a drum track, and he hadn't learned the song. I had to stand up and conduct. He said, 'Can you give me a cue when you get to the middle part?' [...] He hadn't done his homework." Therefore, Entwistle said Moon was "really out of condition" and "disgusted with himself."

7. D. No one knows. Pete once said it was an attack on disco. "With 'Sister Disco," I felt the need to say that the group would never, ever, in any way do

anything like the Bee Gees. We stand over here and what we stand with is all right. They might say we're boring old farts, but we still feel more athome with the boring old farts than any of that crowd." And in another interview, he exclaimed, "It's got nothing to do with disco at all! It's only a series of lines put together. The chorus 'Goodbye Sister Disco, now I go where the music fits my soul'

... that is not an indictment of disco music. I like a lot of disco music; I even like discos." Roger had no idea, and said, "I really like 'Sister Disco' but I don't necessarily understand what he's saying. I do understand what he's trying to say but I don't know whether it comes off." Yeah, we know what you mean, Roger.

8. D. *Grease - Original Soundtrack*. We will not comment.

9. C. They loved it. Editor Ed Rothkowitz previewed clips for the members and their wives. He remembers, "Townshend was on the floor, banging his head. He and Moon were hysterical. Daltrey's wife was laughing so hard she knocked over the coffee table in the screening room. Their reaction was unbelievable. They loved it. That's when they were convinced that the movie was worth doing."

10. A. The Smothers Brothers Comedy Hour. They lip-synched "I Can See for Miles" and "My Generation." Then smashed their instruments as they often did.

However, this mess was so explosive that Pete's hair caught fire, and shrapnel from the drums left a gash in Keith's arm.

11. C. "Pinball Wizard." "Young Man Blues" was recorded at the Colosseum, "My Generation" on the Smothers Brothers Comedy Hour, and "Anyway, Anyhow, Anywhere" on the show Ready, Steady Go.

12. A. The Rolling Stones Rock and Roll Circus. The show was shelved after it was recorded in December 1968. Reportedly, one of the reasons it was shelved was because The Who upstaged them in the performance. Pete liked the Stones, but he said they were off that night. "When they really get moving, there is a kind of white magic that starts to replace the black magic, and everything starts to fly. That didn't happen on this occasion; there's no question about that. They weren't just usurped by The Who, they were also usurped by Taj Mahal — who was just, as always, extraordinary. They were usurped to some extent by the event itself: the crowd by the time the Stones went on were radically festive." It finally came out in 1996, so you can see for yourself.

13. A. *CSI: Crime Scene Investigation. CSI* sure has good taste in opening music. Here is a complete list of The Who songs they have opened shows with: "Won't Get Fooled Again" - *CSI: Miami;* "Baba

O'Reily" - *CSI: New York*; "I Can See for Miles" - *CSI: Cyber*.

14. D. 60. The sessions were insane. Keith's girlfriend at the time, Annette Walter-Lax, says it was "mayhem, total mayhem. I don't know how many producers that he had in the studio, I think it was three. He could smash up the chair once because we couldn't hold a tune. It was a mixture of partying, drinking, taking lots of drugs, and lots of people in the studio, you know, hangers-on, and people showing up. I wasn't in the studio when they were there because I needed some space (laughs), so I was kind of glad to be home alone sometimes. But it was crazy, it was as crazy as the record sounds."

15. False. The two lived together in Santa Monica during the period John calls his "lost weekend." He was there with his girlfriend, May Pang, after separating from Yoko Ono. At the time, John was recording his *Rock 'n' Roll* cover album with producer Phil Spector. Keith poured a bottle of his urine on the console during the sessions. John wrote an angry letter to Spector: "Phil — Should you not yet know, it was Harry and Keith who pissed on the console. Jerry now wants to evict us, or that's what Capitol tells us. Anyway, tell him to bill Capitol for the damage, if any." John concluded, "I can't be expected to mind adult rock stars."

16. B. *The Buddy Holly Story*. Keith didn't particularly want to go and acted strangely and withdrawn the whole time.

17. D. Mama Cass. Musician Harry Nilsson, a close friend of Moon, was concerned that the apartment was cursed. However, Pete reportedly believed that "lightning wouldn't strike the same place twice."

18. True. Keith was playing very badly at the time. One of the bands roadies noted, "After two or three hours, he got more and more sluggish, he could barely hold a drumstick." When they shot the film for the movie *The Kids Are Alright*, Pete says he "was terrified that Keith wouldn't be able to hide his deteriorating condition." Co-producer Jon Astley says, "I do know at the beginning he wasn'tplaying well, and he was all over the place, and they had to sit him down and tell him to get his shittogether. I don't think he was drinking at the time, he was on slimming aid and things like that. In fairness to him, he did get it together on the album,and he plays really well on parts."

19. False. The hotel employee was not hurt. However, he was traumatized. A neighbor had called to complain about the noise from Moon's room. When a staff member showed up to tell him to keep it down, the drummer trapped him in the room and got the hotel manager on the phone before blowing it up. Keith said, "That, dear boy, was noise."

20. B. No. 2. However, the *New Book of Rock Lists* has
him at the top where he belongs.

104

DID YOU KNOW?

- We think of Keith Moon as the ultimate wildman. However, his drug and alcohol consumption was greatly fueled by work-related stress. His girlfriend in the last four years of the drummer's life, Annette Walter-Lax, recalls that he was much calmer when he wasn't working. "Our holidays were lovely, he could relax during these holidays where he went swimming, diving, relaxing; he wasn't drunk. I mean, amazingly enough, he could stop drinking during these periods, holidays, and it was when he came back to the work, The Who, rock, his rock star status, that seemed to be a problem for him. A typical day apart from the holidays with Keith would just be unpredictable. He could wake up, have breakfast, looking for alcohol, drugs and just start to go off on one of his benders, you know … no, I can't say there was such a typical day, he changed from day to day, he could be funny, he could be fun to be with one day and the next day, he could be something totally different." Being Keith sounds exhausting. Walter-Lax says, "It was very, very hard for him. He felt that need to always oblige to make people happy, try and be funny, always be there, never let the audience down, so there was enormous pressure, yes."

- Keith came to Hollywood to pursue an acting career. Annette Walter-Lax says, "This was part of him wanting to go to Los Angeles from the beginning and wanting to pursue an acting career. And he was trying hard to get involved with that, get involved with people, producers, directors, and so forth, and, of course, being Keith Moon. He met the right people as well. I mean, he had all the opportunities. His problem was staying sober. So, it didn't work out very well for him because he showed up drunk to auditions."

- Ironically, Keith's attempts to kick his alcoholism are what ultimately killed him. When the drummer realized he could not play, and the band may fire him, he decided to quit drinking. Moon headed to Malibu, California. He took 32 tablets of clomethiazole, a sedative designed to help with alcohol withdrawal. His girlfriend was with him at the time. She remembers, "I think that he recognized the drunken feeling he got from these tablets, and that's how he came to take too many because he didn't think they were dangerous, plus the fact that he had been given them from the doctor as well."

- Pete had his problems with Keith Moon. But he always profoundly respected him as a musician: "The Who members all had one great facility once we were making music — they *listened*. So many

musicians and band members couldn't do that. It's
the mark of a great musician, even if — like Keith
Moon — he was a drummer who didn't keep time.
He listened very carefully, and what he played fit
my songs perfectly."

CHAPTER 8:

THE LATTER YEARS
OF THE WHO

1. True or False: Kenney Jones, the drummer who replaced Keith Moon, was at the same party asKeith on the night he died.

2. True or False. The movie *Quadrophenia* was dedicated to Keith Moon.

3. Which of these drummers offered to join The Who?
    a. Cozy Powell
    b. Neil Peart
    c. Ginger Baker
    d. Phil Collins

4. In retrospect, what does Roger think about their decision to hire Kenney Jones as drummer for the band?
    a. He was perfect
    b. He wasn't a good enough drummer

  c. He wasn't right for the band
  d. No one could replace Keith

5. When recording *Face Dances*, Pete got to meet one of his musical heroes. Who was it?
  a. Muddy Waters
  b. Thelonious Monk
  c. Marvin Gaye
  d. Jerry Lee Lewis

6. True or False: *Face Dances* was a commercial failure and did not make the Top 20.

7. True or False: *It's Hard* was the band's last album for twenty years, and Rolling Stone magazine deemed it their worst ever.

8. The Who broke up in 1983. How did it happen?
  a. Roger left
  b. Pete left
  c. John left
  d. It was a mutual decision

9. Which band supported The Who in their farewell tour?
  a. Blondie
  b. The Police
  c. The Clash
  d. Talking Heads

10. True or False: The Who's reunion performance at Live Aid was watched by fewer people than the other acts.

11. Kenney Jones did not join the band for their 1989 reunion tour. Why not?
    a. He had other obligations
    b. He wasn't interested
    c. The band fired him
    d. He was injured

12. The last song The Who ever recorded with John on bass was included on an Elton John tribute album. Which song did they cover?
    a. "Tiny Dancer"
    b. "The Bitch is Back"
    c. "The Border Song"
    d. "Saturday Night's Alright for Fighting"

13. The Who played a show merely four days after John Entwistle died. Where did that show take place?
    a. Wembley Stadium
    b. Madison Square Garden
    c. The Hollywood Bowl
    d. The Colosseum in Rome

14. Roger Daltrey was hit in the head by a microphone swung by which British singer, breaking his eye socket?

a. Cliff Richard
b. David Bowie
c. Gary Glitter
d. Tom Jones

15. Looking back at his peers from the classic rock era, Pete has particular disdain for which of these acts?
a. The Beatles
b. Led Zeppelin
c. The Rolling Stones
d. Cream

16. The drummer The Who has played with in recent years is the son of which legendary drummer?
a. John Bonham
b. Ringo Starr
c. Ginger Baker
d. Neil Peart

17. True or False: Like so many of their albums, the 2019 album *Who* peaked at No. 2 in the charts.

18. How often were Pete and Roger in the studio at the same time while recording *Who*?
a. Never
b. 25 percent of the time
c. 50 percent of the time
d. Most of the time

19. True or False: Pete hates The Who.

20. True or False. Pete still denies that Roger and he are friends.

ANSWERS

1. True. It was a party thrown by Paul McCartney after showing *The Buddy Holly Story*.

2. False. Pete thought that would be cheesy and a bad omen. He notes that "Somebody suggested putting 'This film is dedicated to the memory of Keith Moon' on *Quadrophenia*," and I said, you don't need it. You don't need to say it. *Quadrophenia* is Keith Moon. They'd make a tombstone out of it. It should not seem to be a tombstone for Keith — and God forbid, it turns out to be a tombstone for The Who."

3. D. Phil Collins. Phil was pretty unhappy in Genesis at the time and had yet to become a solo star. However, the band had already hired Kenney Jones.

4. C. But also, B. He wasn't right for the band. Roger says, "We just filled the gap and pushed it back into the same slot with a drummer who was quite obviously the completely wrong drummer. I'm not saying he's a bad drummer. I'm not saying he's a bad guy. I didn't dislike the guy, but I just felt he wasn't the right drummer for the Who. It's like having a wheel of a Cadillac stuck onto a Rolls Royce. It's a great wheel but it's the wrong one." Though the band has continued to play ever since, Roger admits,

"Keith was such an extraordinary drummer, to try and replace him was just ridiculous."

5. C. Marvin Gaye. Apparently, Marvin wasn't doing all that well at the time. Pete recalls that "One night, while I sat with Marvin as he negotiated to buy a rock of raw cocaine as big as a tennis ball, I decided to tell him what his music meant to me."

6. False. The album did quite well and reached No. 4 in the Billboard album charts and made No. 2 in the UK (as usual).

7. False. The magazine was surprisingly complimentary, calling it "their most vital and coherent albumsince *Who's Next.*"

8. B. Pete left. However, it was a bit more complicated than that. Pete's life was unraveling in many ways. In particular, he was undergoing a devastating divorce. He was tired of touring and wanted the band to become a studio-oriented one. However, John insisted he would leave if that were the case.

9. C. The Clash. It is yet another testament to the fantastic ability of The Who to remain relevant and respected even by the punk rock elite.

10. True. But not because they didn't want to watch. The satellite cut out in the middle of the performance, just as Roger got to the famous "Why don't you all f-f-fade away" line in "My Generation."

11. A. He wasn't interested. However, the band tried to make it seem like it was their decision. Pete says, "He just lost patience and is now working somewhere else. We're not unhappy about that."

12. D. "Saturday Night's Alright for Fighting."

13. C. The Hollywood Bowl. Pete remembers, "A first Roger and I sat together in a hotel room in California, and I could see that Roger was not just bereft, but also incredibly shocked and unable to function. I thought, 'I'm going to have to make this decision, whether it stops or whether it goes on.'" Townshend said to the crowd: "We understand. We're not pretending that nothing's happened." Daltrey shared his thoughts during the show. "I just wanted to say that tonight we play for John Entwistle," Daltrey said. "He was the true spirit of rock 'n roll, and he lives on in the music we play."

14. C. Gary Glitter. Roger remembers "I broke my eye socket. "I was out for twenty minutes. I did the show with a patch holding my eye in. That is a little bit concerning." Glitter has since been arrested for pedophilia charges. Daltrey says If I'd known what he was into," Daltrey said years later, "I'd have punched his lights out."

15. B. Led Zeppelin. He hasn't had the greatest things to say about The Beatles either. But there is no comparison. Pete detests Led Zeppelin. The guitarist

says, "I don't like a single thing that they have done, I hate the fact that I'm ever even slightly compared to them. I just never ever liked them. It's a real problem to me cause as people, I think they are really really great guys. Just never liked the band. And I don't know if I have a problem, block too, because they, well that became so much bigger than The Who in so many ways, in their chosen field, I've never liked them." Don't sugar-coat it, Pete. What do you *really* think?

16. B. Ringo Starr. Richard Starkey is a wonderful drummer. Also, it is fitting considering the close friendship between Ringo and Keith.

17. True. In the United States, at least. In the UK it reached No. 3.

18. A. Never. Pete and Roger still have trouble working together. However, it is a remarkable album, nonetheless.

19. True. At least if you take him literally. When asked about the 2014 tour, Pete said, "It seemed like a good idea about six months ago, but I hate performing and The Who and touring. But I'm innately good at it, I don't find it hard."

20. False. Tensions are still there, as we can see from the lyrics, "I know you're gonna hate this song. And that's fair. We never really got along!" However, that is just part of the story. We don't

know if its old age is softening him up or if Roger finally got under Pete's skin, but the guitarist made a touching admission. Working together again has "brought us to a genuine and compassionate relationship, which can only be described as love."

DID YOU KNOW

- As if the band hadn't experienced enough tragedy with the death of Moon, in 1979, their show in Cincinnati turned tragic. In a lamentable turn of events, the show's organizers only allowed entry through two narrow doors. This was a real problem since there 18,348 tickets to the show had been sold. When music was heard and started pushing, and people were trampled and shoved against the doors. All told, 11 fans lost their lives. The Who played as usual. Amazingly, the band was not informed of the tragedy until after the show.

- While many classic rock bands suffer from hearing loss, The Who has a worse case than most. Aside from Keith, who seemingly died before the damage accumulated, the founding members all suffer from severe ear damage. Pete Townshend has awful tinnitus (the condition leads to a persistent ringing in the ears) that forced the band to cancel its spring 2010 tour. The guitarist is now forced to use hearing aids in both ears. Meanwhile, towards his death, John Entwistle couldn't hear the rest of the band and could not keep time. Meanwhile, Roger has admitted to using in-ear monitors and lip-reading because, as he put it, he is "very, very deaf."

- Pete got into some hot water for his incredibly insensitive comments about John Entwistle and Keith Moon in a 2019 interview. The guitarist said, "Thank God they're gone," because they were "fucking difficult to play with." He later apologized for the comments and said, "No one can ever know how much I miss Keith and John, as people, as friends, and as musicians. The alchemy we used to share in the studio is missing from the new album, and it always feels wrong to try to summon it up without them, but I suppose we will always be tempted to try. To this day I am angry at Keith and John for dying. Sometimes it shows. It's selfish, but it's how I feel." Pete enjoys being outspoken and he doubtless had a complicated relationship with his bandmates. However, we are sure he misses them deeply. As Townshend explained, "The upside with Keith and John was that on tour and in the studio, we had so much fun," He noted that "playing with them was hard, but both Roger and I spent a lot of time doubled up in joy and laughter, even though we could have benefited from a quieter life sometimes. It was a riot."

CONCLUSION

We don't know what the future holds for Pete and Roger. However, their legacy as members of one of the most significant and most influential rock bands of all time is assured. They have both shown that they are never willing just to toe the line and always have something interesting to say, whether in their music or interviews. We hope you have enjoyed this foray into The Who nostalgia and that it inspired you to dig into their rewarding discography yet again. Don't worry. It never gets old, and it will never die.

Milton Keynes UK
Ingram Content Group UK Ltd.
UKHW020727131123
432470UK00019B/916